"Where Did You Go, Gehazi?"

Steve Price

"Where Did You Go, Gehazi?"

ISBN:0615958745

ISBN-13:9780615958743

Where Did You Go, Gehazi?

DEDICATION

To my wife, Robin.

You didn't have to, but I'm so glad you did.

Where Did You Go, Gehazi?

Publisher: Steve Price
Contact Information: War Hill South
189 W. Athens St
Winder, GA. 30680

Connect at https://www.facebook.com/graceforgehazi

www.warhillsouth.com

Scriptural references taken from King James Bible (KJV) and New International Version (NIV).

"Where Did You Go, Gehazi" contains recollections from the author's experiences. In some cases, names have been intentionally withheld for the privacy of individuals mentioned in the accounts.

Where Did You Go, Gehazi?

CONTENTS

i.   ACKNOWLEDGMENTS

ii. FOREWORD

1.   GOING TO SEE THE KING   Pg. 3

2.   MAKE ROOM FOR THE PROPHET   Pg. 7

3.   STICKS, STONES AND NEW JAW BONES Pg. 11

4.   MUDDY WATER   Pg. 18

5.   CONFUSED, BROKE AND DESPERATE Pg. 22

6.   WHERE DID YOU GO, GEHAZI?   Pg. 25

7.   FRIENDS IN LOW PLACES   Pg.28

8.   WHY SIT HERE UNTIL WE DIE?   Pg.34

9.   RAG DOLL   Pg.39

10. WINDOWS IN HEAVEN   Pg.44

11. SEVEN YEARS   Pg.48

12. JESUS, YOU ARE MY PRIEST   Pg.54

13. I WENT TO GRACE   Pg.58

14. REMISSION   Pg.66

15. VICTORY IN JESUS   Pg.70

    ABOUT THE AUTHOR   Pg.72

Where Did You Go, Gehazi?

To Bishop Thomas Afari and his beautiful wife, Anna, and all of my precious friends in Techimen, Ghana.

Your heart and desire for the presence of God inspired and changed me. I think of you most every day and I miss you all. We share an experience, a miracle, that none of us will ever forget.

I think of you often and miss you tremendously. The miracle that was birthed out of your heart and desire for God inspired and changed me. I am so grateful for what we experienced together.

With love and hope that I will see you again soon,

Pastor Steve

Where Did You Go, Gehazi?

ACKNOWLEDGMENTS

Lynn G. Hammond, always the principal, thank you for the tremendous effort you put into editing my mess.

Don C. Allen, PhD, my pastor and friend, thank you for the gracious words and for seeing past the leprosy.

Final proof editor: Heather Hatcher

Cover art: Don C. Allen and Michael Jeffords

Where Did You Go, Gehazi?

Foreword

From start to finish "Where Did You Go, Gehazi?" by author Steve Price will remind you where the praises of men should be directed. You will journey with Gehazi, servant to Elijah, through his success and failures, and see how this story of redemption from Scripture parallels our own journey. Then you will find, as I did, the need to repent, because this book becomes more of a mirror upon our own misguided efforts than a window of judgment upon another's.

Grab a box of tissues as you walk with these men and discover, as they did, who you are by realizing the place Christ deserves in your life. With this revelation the opulence of king's palaces and even the moments of miracles will pale in comparison to this reminder that we were all created and gifted to glorify God.

--Don C. Allen, PhD
Senior Pastor, The Church @ War Hill

Where Did You Go, Gehazi?

✝

Isaiah 1:18 KJV

Come now, and let us reason together, saith the LORD: though your sins be as scarlet, they shall be as white as snow; though they be red like crimson, they shall be as wool.

GOING TO SEE THE KING

It was just 10 o'clock in the morning, and the temperature was already in the mid-80's. Even though I had awakened early to prepare, my clothing was damp with perspiration and slightly discolored with African dirt. Very soft, fine dirt, like it had been sifted over and over for many years.

We had received an invitation the night before, and now we were standing at the gates of the palace, waiting for the men who would escort us to the King's porch where we would spend about an hour talking to the most powerful man in Techimen, Ghana, King Nana Akumfi. None of us were exactly sure why we had been summoned to meet with the King, but Bishop Thomas Afari, pastor of The Living God Prayer Center in Techimen, told us stories of growing up with the King and that he was a wonderful man.

So we waited, and soon the big black metal gates that opened to the palace courtyard parted. We were led through the square and up a small flight of stairs to a porch where several well-dressed men were seated in a semi circle facing the King's vacant throne. They all rose and greeted us with huge smiles and handshakes. We took our seats and waited a few minutes until the door opened and the King and his wife joined us on the porch.

The King was tall and slender and dressed in beautiful, traditional royal African garments. His wife was similarly dressed and had a lovely smile. She stood to the right of the throne as the King sat down.

Of course, we had all risen and now stood awaiting a gesture from the King to take our seats. After he had positioned himself, he motioned for us to take our places.

I hadn't known what to expect, but my heart was racing, and all the things I had rehearsed to say now seemed terribly inadequate. The thought went through my mind, "What if he's not happy that we are here in his city preaching about Jesus?" I felt a slight tremble in my hands and a little queasy in my stomach.

As my mind settled into what was happening, one of the men stood and began to make his way around the circle, shaking hands and greeting each of us. When he had finished welcoming every man, he turned to stand before the King and, with a humble bow, reached out to the King who took him by the hand. He spoke softly to

Where Did You Go, Gehazi?

the King who responded with a nod of his head and a smile. Then the man returned to his seat. Next, each man took his turn greeting every other man then, as each man faced the king they would spend a few moments of honor and respect before their King. Bishop Thomas and his men took their turns next; the friendship between Bishop Thomas and King Nana Akumfi was undeniable.

When my turn came, I followed the pattern of those who had gone before me and soon found myself face to face with a King.

His eyes were kind and gentle, and his smile was sincere. He reached out his hand; I embraced it, and then I did my best to express my gratitude for the invitation and the hospitality we had been shown.

I had a tear bottle with me, given to me by a dear sister in the Lord before we left America. She had obtained it in Israel a few months earlier and felt that God wanted me to take it to Africa. I hadn't known why until I offered it to the King as a gift, explaining to him what it was and where it came from. His majesty got a stunned look on his face, and for a moment I thought I had made a terrible mistake. Taking the little blue bottle and turning it in his fingers, he told me he had recently been to Israel on a diplomatic mission and that this little tear bottle was a sign from God for him! He said it would be placed among the treasures of his house!

There was no language barrier. His English was

quite good and thick with a British accent, cultural leftovers from the days when Ghana was "The Gold Coast" under British rule.

The King asked me to sit next to him, and I took a seat to his left. He told me that he had heard we were going to be in Techimen again, and he wanted us to hold several days of crusades in the court yard in front of the palace! I was elated! Later, Bishop Thomas told us that, as far as he could remember, no one had been allowed to do that before. The crowds swelled at those meetings into the thousands; at times I couldn't see beyond them. Many were saved as we preached about Jesus during those special days in the King's courtyard.

At first, my ego took off like a rocket, and I could feel the flush of pride in my face. But it soon became apparent that it wasn't me he was interested in. He had a request: "Tell me about Yeboah and the miracle…"

✝

MAKE ROOM FOR THE PROPHET

Elisha held out the staff: "Gehazi, take my staff and run as fast as you can; don't stop or talk to anyone, and when you get to the house, lay my staff upon the face of the child."

As he took the staff, he must have had chill bumps; this was it! A moment that he had been waiting for, a chance to test out the anointing that he believed one day would be passed down to him. It was a double portion of the anointing that had been upon the great prophet Elijah. Elisha wanted the special anointing and had received it on the day that God carried Elijah away in a whirlwind. Elijah had promised Elisha that he would receive the anointing if he saw Elijah when he went up in the chariot of fire. Elisha didn't let Elijah out of his sight for a moment, and he was there to catch Elijah's cloak as it fell to the earth, signifying that the mantle of Elijah's anointing had now been placed on him.

Elisha had been Elijah's servant, the one that poured water on the hands of Elijah. Gehazi was Elisha's servant; would he be the next great prophet of God in Israel?

As Gehazi turned and began to run, he needed

no directions to the Lady of Shunem's house. He had been there before.

The Lady and her husband had built a room onto the side of their house for the prophet to stay whenever he came to Shunem. Little had they known what marvelous things would happen because of their desire to make room for the prophetic voice of God in their lives.

During a stay, Elisha had sent Gehazi to inquire of the Lady and her husband what they might need. They had asked for nothing, so Elisha asked Gehazi for some ideas about what could be done for them. Gehazi told him that they had no children and, even though the Lady and her husband were both too old for children, Elisha prophesied that in about nine months, they would have a son. Despite her initial doubts, nine months later she was holding her son in her arms.

Gehazi remembered that day vividly as he raced toward Shunem. That little baby had grown into a small boy. We don't know for sure how old he was, but he was probably not yet old enough to be working in the fields with his father. The lad had gone into the field where his father was reaping and had begun to complain of a headache. It became so severe that his father had asked a young man to carry his son out of the fields to his mother. The Lady of Shunem held her little boy in her lap until noon when her little promise from God died in her arms and her world began to cave in.

Where Did You Go, Gehazi?

Gehazi approached the house and bounded up the steps to the prophet's chamber. He entered the room and stopped just inside the doorway, his lungs struggling and his heart pounding in his chest as much from the excitement of this opportunity as from the miles he had just run. As his eyes adjusted to the light, he could see the familiar surroundings just the way they had been years before when the little boys' life had begun with a prophetic utterance. There was a small table with a stool and a candlestick, and up against the wall, a bed. On that bed laid the body of a small child, lifeless.

The reality of what was happening began to grip his mind. This was a dead child, the love of a lady and her husband who had not asked for him, but could not stand the thought of living without him. He stopped and prayed to God before he approached the bedside, then proceeded to place the staff on the little boy's face.

What would happen? Surely he would open his eyes, take a deep breath and jump to his feet! Gehazi watched for any sign of life, a twitch, something, anything. Nothing.

Earlier Elisha had known something was wrong when he saw the Lady approaching in a chariot that was being wildly driven to its limit. He had sent Gehazi on toward her to find out what was happening, but she had dismissed his inquiry and pressed past him toward the man of God. Gehazi had tried to push her away from Elisha's feet as she was telling him what had happened to her son, maybe feeling insulted by her seeming lack of confidence in him.

Gehazi still felt the sting of rejection as he waited for a miracle. Why had she not seen that he was a prophet, as well, the next in line for the mighty anointing of God? "What will she think when they get here and I haven't raised her son from the dead? Why isn't this stick working? Why won't he just wake up? This was my moment to shine; why don't I have what it takes?"

Elisha and the Lady of Shunem approached the house, and Gehazi went out to let them know that the child had not awakened. The look in her eyes must have reinforced the words of his crumbling ego: "I am a failure." He stood there with her and watched as Elisha the Prophet went into the room and closed the door. After what may have been hours, the sound of seven little sneezes lifted the broken hearts of a family of faith and healed them all in an instant. Elisha called Gehazi and asked him to call the Lady in to the room where she fell down at Elisha's feet, bowed herself upon the ground, took up her son and left.

Had Gehazi ever noticed that he was always calling the Lady of Shunem for one reason or another on behalf of Elisha the Prophet? This would be his position in her life again, always carrying messages between the Prophet and the Lady of Shunem.

STICKS, STONES AND NEW JAW BONES

I came through the door of the men's dormitory at Beulah Heights Bible College in Atlanta, Georgia feeling like I was the greatest thing since sliced bread. By the way, what was the greatest thing before sliced bread?

Anyway, I had just delivered one of my required timed sermons in Pulpit Speech class, and I was flying high.

During my second year at BHBC, I began taking several evening classes so I could work full time during the day. In the evening Pulpit Speech class were several men whom I considered mighty men of God, pastors of Congregational Holiness Churches and leaders of the denomination of which I wanted to be a part. I wanted terribly to impress them, and that night I felt like I had hit a grand slam.

Timed sermons leave some beginning speakers shaking in their shoes, and I admit I took some pleasure in watching them struggle, but that night the clock ticked seven minutes just for me. I had carefully prepared my outline for a message entitled "Sticks, Stones and A New Jaw Bone".

The idea was simple, taking the text from 1 Corinthians 1:27 - 28, *"but God hath chosen the foolish things of the world to confound the wise; and God hath chosen the weak things of the world to confound the things which are mighty;* [28]*And base things of the world, and things which are despised, hath God chosen, yea, and things which are not, to bring to nought things that are"*. (KJV).

There are things that God chooses to use: sticks, like Moses' staff, Aaron's rod and Shamgar's ox goad, stones, like David's five smooth stones and the rock that brought forth water at Horeb, and new jaw bones, like the one Samson used to slay a thousand men. I had focused on the idea that Samson hadn't waited until he had a proper to weapon to fight with. He simply used what God had provided. If God will use these things, He will use you!

It was anointed, and I had hit all of my marks. The structure, timing and delivery were all right on the money. I still remember the look on the face of our instructor, Dr. Edwards, as he stood in the back of the room grinning as the class erupted with amen's and applause when I finished. That message got me the highest grade in the class. One of the men in the class room told me years later that he has preached that sermon all over the world. I had hopes of being the one that would preach all over the world, and I left that classroom thinking, "This is it, I am on my way to becoming the next rising young star of the preaching

Where Did You Go, Gehazi?

world!"

     I had been endeavoring to preach since I was sixteen. I stood up on a Sunday night in a small church in Oliver Springs, Tennessee and announced my calling to the congregation. The very next Wednesday night, the pastor had me preaching! The message was on faith. I don't remember much of it, but there was a humble response from the congregation, and the young people seemed touched by the effort. I started preaching anywhere I could, and especially enjoyed street preaching. I spent hours in prayer and was zealous about fasting to the point of visible weight loss. I wanted to be anointed, and I wanted God to use me. I set a goal to lead a thousand people to Christ, and had personally prayed with more than a hundred precious souls before I graduated high school.

     I remember a man in his seventies who received Christ in a meeting where I preached in Rittman, Ohio when I was seventeen. It was the first time he had ever asked God to save him.

     I remember the bus load of band students who were telling ghost stories on the trip home after a concert. We were all piled in the back of the bus. I took my turn and told the story of Jesus' death and resurrection with the same drama and intensity that others had used to tell their stories. By the time we got to the school, many were saved. The next week, in the room where the FCA group met, the crowd had gone from a few to standing room only.

I remember the phone call from Matt during my senior year at Wooster High. I was coming in from my job at The Green Leaf Restaurant and when I answered, Matt was on the other end crying hysterically. He felt like he had nothing to live for and was alone somewhere in the city contemplating suicide. I prayed with him and convinced him to meet me in the cafeteria the next day at school. As we sat across from each other, I presented the Gospel to Matt, and with tears flowing down both of our faces, Matt accepted Jesus with hundreds of students looking on. He was the first of thirty-eight who accepted Jesus in the halls and classrooms over the next few months.

I remember being out on bus visitation with a church group in Dayton, Ohio when I found myself separated from the rest of the group. Going house to house, I turned through a gate in a fence to find myself in a yard full of motorcycles and playing kids. My approach to the house received swift attention from a well-known biker club that wasn't thrilled to find an uninvited visitor had entered their yard. I introduced myself and explained why we were in the neighborhood.

I met Little Dan and Little Sue as well as a mountain of a man named Tramp who shared with me that he was awaiting trial for murder. He assured me "it was an accident."

Where Did You Go, Gehazi?

I sat down in the porch and we began to talk about motorcycles, and the Lord's presence began to change the conversation. Sue told me she didn't like the Bible because it was all about men. I opened my Bible to the book of Esther and read some to her.

I eased over to the book of Romans and began to present the Roman Road. Suddenly Tramp began to cry; he laid his head over on my shoulder and asked me to pray for him. I did so with joy and tears. They didn't want me to leave! They even suggested that I ride with them because they needed a preacher! When it was time to go they promised to be ready for church the next day and to let the kids all ride the church bus. We went by to get the kids the next morning and found the house had been abandoned and, from the looks of it, very quickly.

I had experienced the satisfaction that can only come from leading another person to Jesus many times before that night at Bible College. What happened next revealed that even though God had used me, my reasons for wanting to be a preacher were suspicious.

As I headed to my room, I was beaming with pride. I happened to cross paths with Rick, who, by the way, has gone on to become a great pastor and leader in his organization. Rick had a contagious personality and lit up the world around him with a humble joy. He saw the expression on my face; his smile showed a sincere interest in what had me so fired up. He wanted to know what I was so happy about, so I began to tell him about my seven minute masterpiece.

As I continued, his smile slowly faded and eventually wasn't a smile at all. I don't know what I was fishing for. Was it more attention, more affirmation, or more applause? But it was a big mistake. I tried to make it sound like God had just given me the message and had changed the scripture I had taken for my text at the last minute and had somehow received a great revelation that had brought this mighty message to the Kingdom! The problem was earlier in the week, Rick had been in the room while I was working, and he had seen the entire outline. He called me on it right there in the dormitory hall; I had gone from prophesier to prophe"liar" in about ten minutes.

That moment revealed my character to Rick, and though I didn't have the same confrontation with everyone in the class that night, they had all seen it, too. I doubt it was the first time they had seen how thin my character was, but it may have been the first time I saw it in myself. Steve was in it for the wrong reasons.

Yes, I remember those wonderful moments when God used me to help many find faith in Christ, but I also remember another person, a beautiful, nineteen year-old girl named Laurie who had shared a Greyhound bus ride with me from Indianapolis to Chicago. We had been on the same bus since somewhere in Kentucky. She had approached me during a stop and asked if she could sit up front with me. She had fallen asleep in back and been awakened by a guy groping her. I, of course, said yes. I was surprised by the attraction I felt toward her. It was the first time I felt the reality of the stigma of carrying the cross and I struggled terribly with the desire to share with her as I had so many others, but I couldn't or rather, didn't.

I lost the battle of denying myself so that Christ could use me to reach this precious soul for the vainest of reasons: I wanted her to like me. How selfish my motives were in so many ways and sometimes I still see that pitiful old nature in the mirror. I wanted to preach so people would like me and I wanted to hide my faith away when it wasn't convenient or pleasant for the same reason.

We spent more than three hours talking, and I knew she needed to hear about Jesus. We got off the bus in Chicago where I watched her walk away. I never told her about Jesus. My flesh won, and I have spent my life praying that God would send someone to share His love with her. God please save Laurie....

If I had read on to 1 Corinthians 1: 29, *"That no flesh should glory in his presence"*, I might not have come to write this book.

Steve Price

*How can a person live in a land of
miracles and miracle workers and
not believe in the miraculous?*

MUDDY WATER

Being a great man hadn't protected him. Naaman had been used of God to bring deliverance to Syria, but now he needed someone to bring deliverance to him because Naaman was a leper.

What is leprosy? 'A chronic infectious disease caused by a mycobacterium (*Mycobacterium leprae*) affecting especially the skin and peripheral nerves and characterized by the formation of nodules or macules that enlarge and spread, accompanied by loss of sensation with eventual paralysis, wasting of muscle, and production of deformities —called also *Hansen's disease.*' *(Merriam-Webster Dictionary)* In other words, it is a terrible life-altering skin disease.

The people of Naaman's days didn't have such a definition, but they lived with an everyday reality of leprosy and its consequences. The book of Leviticus, Chapter 13, contains a long list of rules concerning the diagnosis and treatment of leprosy, and though leprosy was undoubtedly a medical issue, it was dealt with much closer to Merriam-Webster's second definition: *"a morally or spiritually harmful influence,"* which is why the stigma of contracting the disease went deeper than skin. It would mean a life filled with physical pain as well as scrutiny through the eyes of the Levitical priests, separation from family for weeks or maybe years, being ostracized from society for the remainder of ones life, and possibly death.

For a man of Naaman's stature, the costs were unacceptable. Surely he must have hoped a cure would come through the doctors and physicians of his day, so imagine his surprise when his wife told him what the little Israeli servant girl that worked in their house had suggested. *"And she said unto her mistress, would God my lord were with the prophet that is in Samaria! For he would recover him of his leprosy."* 2 Kings 5:3 (KJV).

Naaman must have latched on to the idea because the suggestion had gotten to the King of Syria, who was probably a good friend of Naaman, and had sent him on a journey with a letter addressed to the King of Israel asking that he arrange for Naaman's healing.

When he left Syria, Naaman took with him ten talents of silver, six thousand pieces of gold, and ten changes of clothes. He was ready to pay a ransom for his healing. There was such a matter-of-fact attitude in the expectations of Naaman and those with him, as if they had no reason to doubt the little girls' story about a prophet in Israel who could heal a leper. It said a lot for the validity of a young person's testimony.

The King of Israel's response seemed just the opposite. He read the letter and seemed to think the burden of the leper's healing was completely on him.

Where Did You Go, Gehazi?

"Then he tore his clothes, and said, 'Am I God, to kill and to make alive, that this man doth send unto me to recover a man of his leprosy?'" 2 Kings 5:7 (KJV).

How can a person live in a land of miracles and miracle workers and not believe in the miraculous?

Somehow Elisha heard what was going on and assured the King that there was no reason to worry. Elisha would show Naaman that there was a prophet in Israel.

Arrangements were made, and Naaman found his way with his men to Elisha's house. The prophet's instructions were less than appreciated by Naaman. *"Go and wash in Jordan seven times, and thy flesh shall come again to thee, and thou shalt be clean."* 2 Kings 5:10 (KJV).

The leper then went on a rant about rivers in Damascus that were better than all the water in Israel. He hadn't come all the way to Israel to take a dip, or seven, in the Jordan River.

Then he left very angry. He had expected Elisha to come out of his house, call on his God, wave his hands in the air and heal him, not tell him to go bathe in the muddy waters of the Jordan. But his servants intervened and gave him some good advice, and Naaman obeyed. Seven dips later, he was a man with a new lease on life.

I just wonder how much I have missed because I

didn't like the simplicity of God's methods.

What do you do when someone has given you something you could never give yourself? How do you say thank you?

Naaman had prepared to give a fortune in sincere gratitude to Elisha, the man of God. Imagine the moment of revelation he must have had when Elisha refused to accept the gifts that he had carried from his home in Syria. He may have even begun to see the price of obedience and the anointing that Elisha maintained. The price this stranger had paid long before Naaman met him, a need to know that man's source, and maybe a need to know the little servant girl's God had been birthed in him. Money had little, if any, meaning here. How do you give gifts to people who already have everything?

Naaman then promised he would never offer sacrifices to another god again. Yes, I believe Naaman received more than healing from leprosy; he had been touched by the Living God. Never the same! Never the same!

✝

CONFUSED, BROKE AND DESPERATE

It probably comes as no surprise to you that I dropped out of Bible College, but how far I fell just might. I found out there was nothing to stop me from falling if I refused to let God's grace catch me. There was no inherent goodness in me, none. I still hear the Dean of Men pleading with me not to leave the school. He said these words, "You can't leave."

The problem was that I had been leaving family and friends behind since I was sixteen, and nobody told me what I could or couldn't do. I hear the Dean's words so differently now. I had no idea that it was God speaking through that precious brother. I would come to know that "You can't leave" means, "If you are going to become who God has called you to be, you can't always do what you want." You must yield to the easy training of Christ's yoke and finish plowing the field in which the seeds of faith will grow. The harvest starts with the yoke.

Two years and thousands of dollars in school bills later, I was confused, broke and desperate. I left school and the church I had been working with and headed out on a disastrous evangelistic journey with one of my friends from college. By the time we headed back toward Atlanta, things had gone from bad to worse. We stopped south of Nashville, Tennessee, and put the last $5.00 we had in the gas tank instead of our stomachs.

For the first time since I had stood up and announced that I felt God was calling me to preach, I had more than doubts about the validity of my calling. I turned to my friend who was as lost as I was and confessed to him, "Marcus, I think I missed it."

During the weeks and months that followed, I began to explore ways to make a living, all the while nurturing a relationship with Robin, the girl who would become my wife. I was miserable at everything I tried, and I struggled to keep enough money coming in to eat and pay for a place to live.

Sweet Robin always managed to come up with enough loose change, taken from her dad's pockets while he was sleeping (thanks Ronnie), to help me with gas and our dates which were usually with other young people from the church where she grew up. Robin's folks had given her a nice car for her sixteenth birthday, which kept us from having to ride around in my fender-less smoke bomb, but the cumulative effect on me was dragging me deeper into depression. I felt like a loser, and I guess I acted like one, too.

Robin and I were married on November 1, 1986. I still don't know why that beautiful girl loved me, and I still wonder why she has stayed with me for more than twenty-five years.

Where Did You Go, Gehazi?

We had our first daughter, Heather, that same year and she was our world. We worked and took care of that beautiful baby girl, but I just couldn't get a grip on who I was and what to do with my gifts and calling. Robin just needed me to be a husband, a father, and a leader. Job set backs, an accident that took months of rehab, and a failed attempt to re-enter ministry had left me with a sense of guilt and failure that haunted me every second and wore on me from every angle. My faith was ineffective and disconnected from its source and we were in trouble in every area of our lives.

We eventually gave up on church and began to spiral into a life that we had not planned. We would spend seven years out of church and away from God.

Where did you go, Steve?

✝

"I just wonder how much I have missed because I didn't like the simplicity of God's methods."

WHERE DID YOU GO, GEHAZI?

Watching Naaman and his men turn toward their homeland after experiencing a marvelous miracle, Gehazi just couldn't believe Elisha had turned down the gifts that Naaman had offered. What could be wrong with accepting what the man so obviously meant to give? Gehazi knew that they could use the money, and some fresh clothes would have been nice, as well. What was Elisha thinking?

Gehazi decided he was within his rights to follow Naaman and take some of what he had offered to Elisha.

Isn't it funny that when people decide that they know better than the leader God has placed in their lives, they very rarely ask for agreement before they act?

As Gehazi ran after Naaman's company, Naaman got down from his chariot and asked Gehazi if everything was alright. Gehazi told him everything was OK, but Elisha had sent him to ask for clothes and money for a couple of young men from the School of the Prophets who had just arrived and needed some help. Naaman couldn't wait to help. He offered more than Gehazi had asked for and sent some of his servants to help carry it all. When they arrived at the house, Gehazi hid the stuff and sent the servants back to Naaman. He went into the house and stood before Elisha who immediately ask him this question: *"Where did you go, Gehazi?"* 2 Kings 5:25 (KJV).

"I didn't go anywhere," was his quick response. But Elisha knew the truth and called him on it: *"My heart went with you when you went."* 2 Kings 5:26 (KJV). The judgment of God appeared swiftly as Elisha spoke the sentence of a life and legacy of leprosy over Gehazi's existence: *"The leprosy therefore of Naaman shall cleave unto thee, and unto thy seed for ever."* 2 Kings 5:27 (KJV).

At first glance this seems like it may have been too harsh for a first time offense. We have all done stupid things and thank God for grace that kept us from getting what we deserved. But maybe this wasn't a first time transgression. There may be evidence in the list of things that Elisha mentions in his scolding of Gehazi:

"Is it a time to receive money, and to receive garments, and olive yards, and vineyards, and sheep, and oxen, and menservants, and maidservants?" 2 Kings 5:26 (KJV).

The money and the garments were part of the current scenario, but what about the olive yards, vineyards, sheep, oxen, menservants and maidservants? This wasn't the first time people had wanted to bless

Where Did You Go, Gehazi?

Elisha for what he had been used of God to do to help them. Gehazi had seen Elisha turn material offerings down many times before, and he had apparently thought it was time to cash in on some of those blessings.

That's the thing about character flaws. They're usually there long before they cause catastrophic failure.

Gehazi went out from Elisha's presence "a leper as white as snow."

That's it, the end of the dream. I'll never be the great man of God that I thought I would be. The real me is covered from head to toe with an incurable disease that will be with me and my family forever. It had all seemed within reach, and I blew it.

Gehazi and I have a lot in common. End of story.

"That's the thing about character flaws. They're usually there long before they cause catastrophic failure."

✝

FRIENDS IN LOW PLACES

We don't know how long Gehazi was away from Elisha, but we do know that several stories take place in 2 Kings, Chapters 6 and 7, and Gehazi isn't mentioned. Another nameless servant is with Elisha, but Gehazi is just not there. Elisha continued to do great miracles, and God used him mightily. The double portion anointing was working.

Where did you go, Gehazi?

Probably straight to a leper camp. That's where he belonged, right? Do not pass go; do not collect $200.00. He probably didn't even go through the effort of seeking out the judgment of a priest. Of course, that matches the manner of Gehazi's character. Obeying the Word hadn't been part of the process of becoming the next great prophet, so why would it be now?

If we don't allow the Word to judge us at all times, when we're doing well and when we're not doing so well, we may judge ourselves. Self condemnation may set in and drive us further away from the healing power of God's amazing grace.

So off he went covered in rags to hide his

condition, but even the rags declared the plight of what was hidden within. Unclean! Unclean! Even his nightmares were filled with the face of the prophet and the sound of his words, but the images weren't even true anymore. He couldn't really remember his true countenance or the timbre of his voice. Guilt, shame and condemnation had twisted them into a gruesome unloving fiend, bent on tormenting him forever.

The human imagination, left wide open to the enemy, has robbed many souls of the truth of God's grace and mercy. If we could only see ourselves the way the Father does.

"So, you were Elisha's protégé? Pardon me, but if that's true, why didn't he just heal you?"

It was probably hard to answer a question like that, particularly when it was coming from someone who was suffering with the same disease. How would you tell them, "He didn't heal me because he spoke it upon me; he gave it to me because I was an idiot." How do you make friends in a place like this?

Stories that create bonds of kinship somehow warm us as we tell of our life and loves. Of the things that we hoped for and the dreams we had. Of sitting around the fires of a wretched camp, reliving our own Glory Days as others told of theirs and weeping as each shared how leprosy had invaded, torn and slashed its way into their world and sent it all crashing down. Yes,

Where Did You Go, Gehazi?

you were my friend, my companion in an encampment that none of us chose. Well, except Gehazi.

I eventually began using my musical talents in bars and clubs, and occasionally, people would find out that I was a backslidden preacher. And when they would hear how I had made stupid choices and lost the opportunity that God had presented to me, it never brought tears to their eyes or made them raise a glass of cheer to say, "We understand brother; you are one of us!" It usually made them behave like they were hanging around with a backslidden preacher, which is uncomfortable.

The men in Jonah's boat understood this situation. Things always seem troubled and stormy around a person who is running from God. "We think you're a really nice person, but you're making us sea sick." Eventually, they just have to throw you overboard.

Our band had been playing frequently at a small bar near Roswell, GA, and the regular customers had taken us in as their band. The crowds were growing, and our lead singer, Bill, had a knack for stoking the party to a feverish pitch. We used to joke that he had graduated from UGA with a degree in Partying. During a break between sets one Friday night, a young man and his girlfriend approached me and asked if they could talk with me for a few minutes. I said sure, and we settled into the booth that was reserved for the band.

"We want to know if you will marry us." I think I must have looked like I had seen a ghost as they stared at me with eyes wide and grins from ear to ear. They asked me again, and I, in turn, asked them why they wanted me to marry them. They told me they had heard I was a preacher, and since they didn't have a church or a pastor, I was IT. I respectfully declined and offered some suggestions on where they could find a real preacher.

That was the night I realized what my story must have sounded like to the guys who were closest to me and that the anointing and calling of God are without repentance.

Spending time with Jesus has a lifelong effect. What is hard to get your mind around is this, even when you are wrong, He is right. When you are un-holy, He is Holy. When you are weak, He is strong. The stains of His blood do not wash out of one's soul easily. I think I talked about Jesus all the time. Really, He was all I thought about. The band members had heard all about what I almost became during our long hours of practice and studio sessions. Those stories caused them to have respect for me and my wife. They even kept women at bay because they honored our marriage. I was cool to have around because I rarely drank to excess, and they could usually count on me to be the dedicated driver. But the downside was that when they wanted to do songs that dishonored God, I wouldn't agree. It limited our song selection considerably, and some saw me as weight they didn't want around.

Where Did You Go, Gehazi?

Eventually, I had to get out of their boat. I do want to honor the beauty of God's grace here, though.

When I first met Bill, our lead singer and guitarist, I was blown away by his talent and taken back to find that he was basically agnostic. I couldn't believe how well our talents worked together, and we wrote some beautiful songs. We had come very close to a tour agreement with a well-known recording company that would have taken us out West. We would have been on the road without my wife and daughter for several months. But all of that changed, and my world was filled with a clarity and direction I had seldom experienced when my wife called to tell me we were expecting our second child. I made the best choice I had made in many years. I chose to quit the band and be there for my wife and my kids.

Bill tried to understand my decision, but it was hard for him. Several weeks after I left the band, Bill met me at a restaurant to discuss ownership rights to the music we had written and to clear the air between us.

I was amazed when I realized that God had joined our meeting that day!

We were sitting on the deck just doing business when the conversation turned personal. Bill began to tell me that he had come to believe in God because of my stories and the way I loved my family. Suddenly, we both began to cry, and Bill was laughing and crying at the same time. The presence of God was so strong! I prayed with Bill as he declared his faith in Jesus on the deck of a restaurant with dozens of people watching.

Remember, Jonah's shipmates had a little talk with God when he left their boat, as well.

God has a way to bring us back into His will. Sometimes it takes a ride in the belly of a whale to get us there, but He has a way.

✝

WHY SIT HERE UNTIL WE DIE?

The city of Samaria had been under siege by the Syrians long enough for things to get really bad. Bad enough to raise the value of things like donkey heads and dove dung, bad enough for two women to agree to eat their own babies. Bad enough for the King of Samaria to put on sackcloth underwear and declare he would kill the Prophet Elisha.

Hunger. It makes people do crazy things, and this was a hungry city.

Elisha stepped out in the open even though the King had declared he wanted his head cut off and declares.

"Hear ye the word of the Lord; tomorrow about this time shall a measure of fine flour be sold for a shekel, and two measures of barley for a shekel, in the gate of Samaria." 2 Kings 7:1 (KJV).

Ok, I stink with money, but I can figure this out. Supply and demand is about to kick in, and in this case, supply is about to drive prices way down. Flour and barley will be so abundant in twenty-four hours that they will be sold dirt cheap in a city so hungry they would give anything for flour and barley today.

One of the king's right hand men retorted,

> *"Behold, if the Lord would make windows in heaven, might this thing be?"* Elisha responded to his doubt, *"Behold, thou shalt see it with thine eyes, but shalt not eat thereof."* 2 Kings 7:2 (KJV).

This man had been given charge of the gate and a day later that man was trampled to death when the people of the city stormed the gates having learned that God had delivered them from the enemy's bondage and given them the enemies' camp, full of food and supplies. Elisha's prophecy was fulfilled. That man saw it, but he never tasted a bite.

So how had this happened?

Even a starving city can't afford to let lepers wander the streets, so outside the walls of Samaria, four leprous men waited and hoped that somebody on the inside would have compassion on them and toss some bread over the wall. But day after day the people became more desperate, and the odds that someone would help them became less likely.

We have no measure of the scope of the relationship between these lepers. They shared a common bond, they shared a common need, they shared a common place, but one of them had something else…insight into their situation that had the power of

Where Did You Go, Gehazi?

the prophetic anointing behind it.

As I read the story, I can't help but ask if they heard what Elisha had boldly proclaimed within the walls of Samaria? I don't know. But it could have been the other way around. Maybe Elisha had heard the conversation that had taken place between the lepers. Maybe the Lord had been waiting for them to make some decisions about their situation and had spoken to Elisha that the time of deliverance had come. I just can't separate the events. One triggered the other.

One of the lepers had come to the conclusion that Samaria wasn't going to help them. He said, "Why do we sit here until we die? We can't go into the city because there is nothing there for us, so let's go to the enemy's camp and hope for mercy. The worst they could do is kill us and we are surely going to die if we stay here."

So, they got up and started toward the enemy's camp. Maybe that was the moment Elisha was waiting for! Is it possible that in the midst of our desperation there are the ingredients of a marvelous move of God that could bring salvation not only to us, but to many who are starving for the Word of God in a world just a wall away? Have we been waiting for God to move while He was waiting for us to move? Why do we sit here until we die? Had these unwanted, thrown away lepers ignited the Word of Prophecy that would save thousands?

Steve Price

So, down the road they went! And as they went, God went with them. Somehow, God began to amplify the sound of their footsteps. I enjoy imagining that it was thousands of angels that had come to walk alongside them as they marched into the unknown! It sounded like an army marching toward the enemy's camp!

Child of God, you are not alone in that moment when you step out by faith! When everything seems to be against you and all you know to do is get up and move. When you say, I don't know what tomorrow holds, but I absolutely refuse to sit here until the devil has robbed me of everything! I'm going to the enemy's camp, and I'm taking back what the devil has stolen from me! Remember His name! Emmanuel, God is with us!

Either way, the enemy heard them coming and became convinced that Samaria had somehow gotten help from one of their allies. By the time the lepers got to the camp, the enemy was gone! They had become so afraid of the sound of that four man army that they had left everything, even left the fires burning, and ran for their lives.

The lepers approached the camp cautiously, trying to get some idea of how to approach the populace in their bid for maybe a little something to eat. As they hunkered down behind nearby bushes, the camp was eerily quiet. Fires burned, animals stood around, and tents full of unguarded supplies awaited possession by their new owners. After some time they mustered the courage to begin looting the tents near the edge of the camp, and after they faced no opposition, began to boldly run from tent to tent, giddy and drunk with the knowledge that their wildest dreams hadn't prepared them for this. They had hoped for a dew drop and had gotten the outpouring!

"My God shall supply all my need according to His riches in Glory by Christ Jesus!" Philippians 4:19 (KJV).

Steve and Yeboah

RAG DOLL

As a preacher, you get used to distractions of all kinds during the delivery of a message. A sneeze that sounds funny, a baby crying, elderly sisters carrying on a conversation that they think no one else can hear. I was once the pastor of a church that was so close to the train tracks we could feel the floor shake as each one came by, and we had many laughs listening to recordings of the sermons and hearing the whistle blow at the worst of times.

But none of them ever prepared me for the distraction of a desperate mother trying to get her dying child into a church service. It might have been like the sound of a roof being ripped open so the friends of a dying man could lower him down to the only hope he had (Mark 2:1-12).

The crowd rustled with sudden movement, and voices in their native tongue rose from the back of the room. Some sounded stern and angry, while others sounded pleading and desperate. After a moment, the pleading voices must have convinced the angry to understand why they were there, and the crowd opened enough for a mother, along with a couple of friends, to carry the frail, limp body of her ten year-old daughter to a row of seats on the right side of the building.

Those who were seated quickly gave place to this weary family. They had traveled from the city of Accra and made the arduous journey to Techimen as they nursed a beautiful child that was literally dying. From what we gathered, a disease had attacked the little girl's spinal cord just below the base of her neck, and she had been losing functionality of her limbs and organs. It had come suddenly and ferociously.

The family had taken her to the hospital in Accra where there would be a much better chance that she might get the care she needed. They had been terribly disappointed to find out that what help was there would be too little, too late. The doctors had instructed them to take her home and prepare for her funeral.

As they made their way north from Accra, they heard a radio advertisement announcing a Leadership Seminar and Crusade to be held in Techimen, Ghana. The event dates were October 12th – 15th, 2005, with Crusade services nightly at the Nyame Tease Prayer Center, and daily leadership training at the Agyeiwaa Hotel.

It was during the first leadership meeting that we were introduced to the leaders who had come in from all over Ghana, as well as Cote d'Ivoire, Burkina Faso and Togo. We were exhausted from the journey which had

Where Did You Go, Gehazi?

started with a red eye from Atlanta, a six hour layover in London, and an eight hour flight to Ghana where we experienced visa issues that caused us to miss our arranged in-country transportation. We spent a couple of hours making new travel arrangements, which amounted to a seven passenger van that was missing all the padding on the seats, and was packed with twelve people whose luggage was strapped precariously on top.

We had traveled for several hours along roads that looked like they had been rutted with massive rains, and made a stop in Kumasi to find another equally challenged van to take us the rest of the way into Techimen, the heart of Ghana.

I was so tired by the time the sun began to rise that all I wanted to do was get to the hotel and get some sleep.

When I say hotel, please don't envision an American hotel. It was the best accommodations our precious friends in Techimen could have found for us, and it was more than enough for the job we were there to do, but it was no Hilton.

As the young men who had been assigned to help us were carrying our luggage to the rooms, they informed me that the first leadership training would begin at 9:00. It was already near 7:00. I had two hours to freshen up and make my way to the conference room. I think I was literally shaking from exhaustion by the time I took the podium.

It was late into the session when the commotion began as they brought the little girl into the room, and I knew something was happening of which God was solely in charge . I have come to recognize the value of agenda modification as it is directed by the Holy Spirit. It pretty much goes like this: If He is moving, get out of His way.

I had already determined to end promptly at noon as advertised, and I would have cut the meeting short due to our travel fatigue if there had been time to catch up the planned training material in a later meeting. But God had other plans.

As I neared dismissal of the 100 plus leaders gathered there, Bishop Thomas came and spoke into my ear that we needed to pray for this little girl. We pressed toward the side of the room where this distraught mother sat with a weak little girl who lay on a blanket in the floor in the same position she had been in since they had arrived.

I will never forget the first time I looked into her eyes. They were full of thought and intelligence and were obviously screaming, "Please help me." She was unable to move anything except her eyes and her mouth as she tried to speak, and she hadn't been able to swallow in days. She was limp as a dish rag, so we had nicknamed her "Rag Doll".

Where Did You Go, Gehazi?

We began to pray, anointing her with oil, and the sound of prayer in that room was like nothing I had ever heard in a church service in all of my life. Long, fervent, passionate, prayer. I realized that I was no match for these warriors of intercession, and I would learn from them through that week what the effectual, fervent prayer of the righteous sounds like. Pray quietly if you must, but it's just not the kind of praying that I do much of anymore. I felt the presence of the Holy Spirit so strong that I thought I would fall to the ground!

But after the prayer had subsided, I, with my "need to see it" eyes of faith, or lack thereof, watched for some sign that a miracle was manifesting. Judge me if you must, but I was thinking, "This would sure get this crusade off to a great start if that little Rag Doll gets up and walks!"

She didn't move anything except those eyes.

We would pray for her five times over the course of the next three days. But we would find out on Friday night that it wasn't prayer for the Rag Doll that would leave us broken and changed forever in the manifestation of the delivering power of God's love. It would be prayer for her mother.

Steve Price

Yeboah and her Mother

Where Did You Go, Gehazi?

✝

WINDOWS IN HEAVEN

Inside the city of Samaria, rumors spread that the Prophet Elisha had really stepped in it this time. He had prophesied yesterday that the famine would come to an end, and his time was about up. Skeptics and doubters of all kinds prepared their "I told you so" speeches. Others, full of hope from his words, now clung to the few minutes left before Elisha would be dragged out and publicly executed. Many blamed him for their troubles anyway. This was his just desserts.

As they languished through another desperately long day of hunger, four unwanted, social outcasts were lying back on the spoils of their enemies, full of good food and pockets laden with more treasure than they could carry.

I study those around us who are affecting their sphere of influence both positively and negatively. They are leaders. Leaders gifted to impact the two or three friends around them or the masses that attend the churches where they pastor. Leaders with the power to sway opinion or even dictate belief of all kinds. Sometimes they use the gift as a means to manipulate scenarios for their own selfish gains. You hear about them all the time.

But then there are those who see the bigger purpose of the gift and carry it humbly, utilizing its power to bring others into miracles they couldn't gain on their own.

This was the kind of leader who was among the four lepers, now all very rich, who had insight into why the abundance had been given to them. It was probably the same leper who had the prophetic insight into their situation only a few hours earlier and raised the question," Why do we sit here until we die?"

In a moment of true clarity of purpose, he looked at his brothers in rags and said these words:

"We do not well. This day is a day of good tidings and we hold our peace" 2 Kings 7:9 (KJV).

"Why would we share this blessing with the people who cast us out and treated us like we were dogs? Why take a chance on them taking everything we have gotten by our efforts?" Those thoughts apparently never entered their minds. They got up and went to the gate of Samaria and begin to cry out the good news: "God has made a way where there seemed to be no way! Go tell the King that the enemy is defeated!"

I don't believe I can begin to write this part any better than it is written in 2 Kings 7:10 -20:

Where Did You Go, Gehazi?

"They (the 4 lepers) came and called unto the
porter of the city: and they told them, saying, We came
to the camp of the Syrians, and, behold, there was no
man there, neither voice of man, but horses tied, and
asses tied, and the tents as they were.

And he called the porters; and they told it to the king's
house within.

And the king arose in the night, and said unto his
servants, I will now show you what the Syrians have
done to us. They know that we be hungry; therefore are
they gone out of the camp to hide themselves in the field,
saying, When they come out of the city, we shall catch
them alive, and get into the city.

And one of his servants answered and said, Let some
take, I pray thee, five of the horses that remain, which
are left in the city, (behold, they are as all the multitude
of Israel that are left in it: behold, I say, they are even as
all the multitude of the Israelites that are consumed:)
and let us send and see.

They took therefore two chariot horses; and the king
sent after the host of the Syrians, saying, Go and see.

And they went after them unto Jordan: and, lo, all the
way was full of garments and vessels, which the Syrians
had cast away in their haste. And the messengers
returned, and told the king.

And the people went out, and spoiled the tents of the

Syrians. So a measure of fine flour was sold for a shekel, and two measures of barley for a shekel, according to the word of the LORD.

And the king appointed the lord on whose hand he leaned to have the charge of the gate: and the people trode upon him in the gate, and he died, as the man of God had said, who spake when the king came down to him.

And it came to pass as the man of God had spoken to the king, saying, Two measures of barley for a shekel, and a measure of fine flour for a shekel, shall be tomorrow about this time in the gate of Samaria:

And that lord answered the man of God, and said, Now, behold, if the LORD should make windows in heaven, might such a thing be? And he said, Behold, thou shalt see it with thine eyes, but shalt not eat thereof.

And so it fell out unto him: for the people trode upon him in the gate, and he died" (KJV).

I wonder what doubting God's Word has cost me?

Where Did You Go, Gehazi?

SEVEN YEARS

It had been seven years. That's how long Robin and I had been away from the church. The first seven years of our marriage, give or take a few attempts to clear our conscience and make a showing at some old friends' events, weddings, funerals, and so, was long enough for the church to have changed a lot since we had been involved as teenagers. It had also been long enough for contemporary gospel music to have taken hold, and gone were the days of elderly sisters sticking their fingers in their ears while I attempted to belt out Don Francisco's, "He's Alive." My electric guitar was welcome on the platforms of churches everywhere we went, and even the Southern Gospel group I had teamed up with was incorporating the heavy distortion that I loved into the toe-tapping songs we were performing. Robin would tag along with our seven year-old daughter, Heather and her baby sister, Courtney, and we would ride for hours to any little church that would give us a chance to play and sing. I was enjoying my life, leprosy and all.

When we began to come back to the Lord, we didn't have a church to call home. Everywhere we went just seemed a bit alien, and maybe we had lost our churchy skills or just remembered what church used to be like, but we longed for the long hours of tarrying in the altars and praying for one another until we broke through. We began to watch every TV evangelist we could and began studying the Word and praying, occasionally inviting the band mates over for Bible study and prayer meetings. We even began to send our tithe and offerings to whomever we felt God was speaking to us about.

It was during this time that we went to visit Robin's parents who had sold the home where Robin grew up in Decatur, GA, and had moved out into the suburbs to Buford. They had found a lovely home in a beautiful neighborhood, and we would make the trip from Alpharetta to visit them nearly every weekend.

Robin and I had never been good with money, and we hadn't saved much or planned for more than living from paycheck to paycheck, but Robin longed for a home of our own where we could raise our little girls. She and her mom would get in the car during our weekend visits and ride through the quickly-growing communities around where her parents lived and come back full of stories of beautiful starter homes that they were sure we could afford. I would listen, but inwardly I was saying, "Sure, if God made windows in heaven and poured out houses, we might have a chance to get one."

Then, one Sunday afternoon, after hours of house exploration, Robin came in and began her exposition of the great places they had seen, and one in particular had caught her attention. They had even spoken to the real estate agent on site, and she was convinced she could get us in one of the homes that were under construction. I prepared to begin my usual "Yeah, but" speech when I caught a look in Robin's eyes that made me stop and think for a moment. I heard God say to me, "I want more for you than you want for yourself, and I want you to stop trying to pay for your mistakes with misguided self sacrifice. Listen to your wife..."

She had braced herself for my objections, but instead I said, "Let's go take a look." She lit up! And in a few minutes, we were all making the nine mile trip from my in-laws' house to a little house in Barrow County.

As we climbed out of the car and began to walk up the driveway, I breathed out these words, "Lord, Your will be done," and after a walk through the unfinished home, I was convinced this would become our first house. And it was more than I had ever dreamed that we could have.

We went to the real estate office, put down $500.00 earnest money and signed a contract. A few months later, I carried my wife over the threshold into our first home, and it became the place where we would live and love, laugh and cry, for the next twelve years.

It's amazing what seven years had done for

Gehazi, as well. He had gone from the obscurity of failure to an audience with the King of Samaria.

Shortly after the great events that had brought deliverance to the great city through the valor of four lepers, a famine had come upon the land that would challenge the entire nation to survive.

Elijah had warned the Lady of Shunem that she needed to go find a way to survive the famine anyway she could, so she had taken her family and sought refuge amongst the Philistines until the famine had passed and she could return home.

As she returned to her home in Shunem, she found it had been taken over, and she had no power to evict the squatters who now held the ground that belonged to her and her family.

She made her way to Samaria with the hope of getting the King to help her. As she approached the throne room, the King was having a conversation with an unlikely sort of man. The discussion was centered on a question the King had asked him: "Tell me about Elisha and the great things that he has done." As the man was telling the King about the time Elisha had raised a dead body, the Lady of Shunem interrupted the exchange.

As she raised her voice, begging the King's help, Gehazi looked at the King in astonishment and said, "Oh King! That is the woman I was just telling you about, and that is the son that Elisha raised from the dead!"

The King must have been overwhelmed at what God had done to cause such a convergence of history and drama! He immediately appointed an officer to take the woman and her family and restore unto her all that belonged to them!

I doubt the Lady looked upon Gehazi the way she had years ago in those desperate, troubled moments when she was seeking Elisha to intervene on behalf of her dead son.

Gone were the doubts and misgivings about a young man with character problems, and even though the scars of failure clung to his skin, there must have been a wonderful acknowledgement of gratitude that this man's broken road had led him to a place where he now interceded on her behalf before the King. She may not have known how he had managed to make it to the throne of the King, but she probably didn't care, and Gehazi could only rejoice in this. He hadn't been able to help her before his skin had been riddled with the leprosy of sin. But now, he could help her because he had found access to the King.

Wow! Talk about being in the right place at the right time. The question is, how did a leper get an audience with the King? What was he doing there? There is one thing for sure; those around the King wouldn't have let just any leper into the presence of their King. What if he were contagious and the King became a leper, as well? It could be disastrous for the kingdom. Of course, this leper was probably the voice of reason that seven years earlier had spoken in harmony with the prophetic utterance of Elisha when he asked, "Why do we sit here until we die?" It was probably this leper who had humbly brought an answer to the call of responsibility as he led his fellow neighbors into the abundant gratefulness that would be forever theirs with these words of wisdom, *"We do not well, this is a day of good tidings and we hold our peace"* 2 Kings 7:9 (KJV).

But even with that, a contagious leper in the presence of your King is a dangerous thing to risk. Why would the King's guards take such a chance?

He must have gone and shown himself to the priest. That's why.

JESUS, YOU ARE MY PRIEST

Biblical accounts of leprosy are not limited to the Old Testament. Jesus has several encounters with lepers in the Gospels, and each time His instructions were the same.

"But go, and show thyself to the priest, and offer for thy cleansing, according as Moses commanded, for a testimony unto them" Luke 5:14 (KJV).

Jesus was referring to the rules of Leviticus, chapter 13, that contained the parameters of diagnosis and various degrees of control and containment for those who were afflicted with leprosy. In the somewhat difficult set of laws, one thing is clear: it is the way the priest sees you that will determine your destiny.

In the story of the ten lepers in Luke, chapter 17, Jesus answers the anguished cry of a band of leprous men. He didn't pray that their leprosy be removed, He instructed them to go show themselves to the priests. The part that would have been hard for the ten men to obey was this; they had probably been to the priests when they were initially diagnosed and summarily banished and, at the moment, they could look at their skin and see that nothing had changed. So the first few steps for them would have been with some trepidation.

They started the journey back to the judgment seat where they had received the sentence of exile, but now with a renewed hope because of the voice of the one who was sending them. This was the voice of Jesus, the one who was healing the sick and raising the dead, and now He had heard them and spoken to them! All they had to do was obey.

As they went, they began to see the healing taking place in one another. Imagine the shouts of joy as they pointed to each other's once horrid condition and began to declare, "You're clean! You're clean!"

As we have each heard the voice of Jesus calling us into a journey of faith with a destination called "Clean," would it not be better if we looked at one another and began to point out the changes that faith is having in us rather than continually reminding each other, and ourselves, of what we used to be? When you have spent every day just hoping that you would see a change for the better you better believe it brings shouts of joy and praise to the Lord when it happens in dramatic fashion! We should rejoice in the change that has come since Jesus declared over us, *"You are already clean because of the word I have spoken to you"* John 15:3 (NIV).

Where Did You Go, Gehazi?

I see Christ at work in you!

In the midst of the celebration, one of the former unclean stopped, and, as the others continued hurriedly toward the declaration of cleansing from the priests, light and truth filled his soul.

"Go show yourself to the priests."

He turned and looked back up the road where the Lord stood watching them as they went, and he began to run back toward Jesus as fast as he could.

All he could think about were those words, "Go show yourself to the priests."

I will do just that! I will show myself to the Priest!

As he neared Jesus, he fell to the ground and began to worship Him! The revelation had brought him into a place of wonderful worship.

Jesus is my Priest!

See the words of Hebrews 2: 14 – 17:

[14]Forasmuch then as the children are partakers of flesh and blood, he also himself likewise took part of the same; that through death he might destroy him that had the power of death, that is, the devil; [15]And deliver

them who through fear of death were all their lifetime subject to bondage. ¹⁶For verily he took not on him the nature of angels; but he took on him the seed of Abraham. ¹⁷Wherefore in all things it behooved him to be made like unto his brethren, that he might be a merciful and faithful high priest in things pertaining to God, to make reconciliation for the sins of the people" (KJV).

"Where are the other nine?" On their way to try to get the approval of religion or the affirmation of men. Attempting to ascend to the knowledge of Christ surely brings lifestyle modification but may leave the true treasure waiting to be discovered at the Lord's feet.

There are those that, despite the change that has taken place in us, will refuse to give us the words that we need to set us free.

Your dad may never say the words you desperately need to hear, "I'm proud of you." Your mom may never hold you close and tell you, "I love you unconditionally."

But there is one who waits for you to realize who He is, and He longs not only to give you healing but to give you life more abundantly!

How we miss the fullness of His work in us when we limit it only to the work it does in reconciling us to our broken lives. At the feet of Jesus this one stranger found more.

Where Did You Go, Gehazi?

"And he said unto him, Arise, go thy way: thy faith hath made thee whole." Why settle for "clean" when "whole" is an act of sincere worship away?

Jesus, you are my Priest!

"WHERE ARE THE OTHER NINE?" ON THEIR WAY TO TRY TO GET THE APPROVAL OF RELIGION OR THE AFFIRMATION OF MEN. ATTEMPTING TO ASCEND TO THE KNOWLEDGE OF CHRIST SURELY BRINGS LIFESTYLE MODIFICATION BUT MAY LEAVE THE TRUE TREASURE WAITING TO BE DISCOVERED AT THE LORD'S FEET.

✝

I WENT TO GRACE

The prayer meeting had begun at 4:00 at Nyame Tease Prayer Center, and by the time we arrived at 6:00 the place was nearly full.

The way Bishop Thomas had taught the people to pray was powerful. Daily prayer meetings would begin with a few folks led by one of the dozens of men who were committed to the ministry and had placed themselves under Bishop Thomas' leadership. They would ask the Lord to speak to them about what prayers they should lead, then they would instruct the people concerning the direction they felt the prayer should go and what the target would be. The leader would begin to pray long and loud, and the people would join in. A single targeted prayer might last for ten minutes or more. The prayer leader would be responsible for about an hour of this corporate, targeted prayer.

The transition between prayer leaders would be filled with songs, and the crowd would grow steadily through the three hours preceding the 7:00 service.

When we came out of the back office on that Friday night to what I thought would be just another night of singing and preaching, the church was praying at a feverish level.

I have always considered myself to be above average when it comes to demonstrative worship, but I felt nearly overwhelmed by the intensity of the people's intercession. I had never seen anything like this.

I went to my seat on the platform, sat down in my chair and tried to get my mind around what I was hearing and seeing. The atmosphere was electrified! I tried to join in, but kept sinking into the realization that I didn't know how to pray. Not like this.

Our interpreter was sitting to my right, and he was literally leaning on my shoulder, speaking into my ear so I could hear him. After awhile I asked him to stop, and I knelt down on the floor and began to sob. I was being taught what prayer can be, and it was convicting me. Lord, teach me to pray.

The crowd had grown through the hours to fill the Prayer Center to capacity, and the Holy Spirit was there, leading all that was happening.

I don't remember what was preached or how it came to be that the altars were full of people seeking God, but I do remember the moment the miracle began.

As I mentioned earlier, we had prayed for Yeboah in every service since she had arrived on our first day there, but had seen no change in her. The family had chosen to stay in the Prayer Center the entire time they were there, as had many others. Every night after service, mats that were piled against a wall would be spread across the floor, and they had slept there. They were desperate for God to intervene and were willing to do whatever it took to be there when the miracle came.

So this night seemed to be on the same path. We would get to a point where someone would come and lead us through the crowd to where Yeboah's limp frame was lying in the floor on one of those mats. We would pray for her and hope for the miracle, but this night would be different.

In the book of Acts, chapter 16, we find the story of Paul and Silas after they had been arrested for delivering a young woman from a spirit of divination. They had been thrown into the inner part of the jail, and their hands and feet had been bound in stocks.

At midnight, they began to pray and sing praises to God, worshipping Jesus. As they worshipped, there came a great earthquake that shook the prison to its foundations, opened the doors and loosed the chains of everyone! The jailer came running and was going to kill himself because he was sure the prisoners would have escaped. But Paul told him not to hurt himself because no one had fled, they were all there. The event was so powerful that the jailer and his entire family were saved and baptized!

The Word makes a point in verse 25 that the

prisoners were listening. Why is that significant?

When we're in a bad spot, it's so easy to fall into complaining or worrying, many times saying and doing things that are contrary to our faith. The prison doesn't shake, and the chains don't come off when we fail to worship the Lord during those moments, and it's sad that we spend so many hours entangled in those traps. If the devil can convince us there's no power in the name of Jesus that will break chains and loose bondages, he can keep us locked up in depression, anger, resentment, etc. for way too long.

But when we learn that worship and declaring the name of Jesus during every circumstance of our lives will bring freedom, the chains fall off and the doors are opened!

What we must remember is that the prisoners are listening. We're usually not alone when we're venting our frustrations. Lost husbands and wives are listening. Our children are listening. Family members, desperate for answers, are listening. They are all waiting for us to truly respond to what we say we believe.

If we would learn to worship the Lord on the mountains and in the valleys, good times and bad, we would begin to see those around us find freedom through the power of Jesus' name!

That's what happened the night Yeboah received her miracle. I can honestly say I'm glad it wasn't through my hands. I was just blessed to be there when it came.

As we moved through the crowd praying for them, I noticed Yeboah was lying in the floor alone. As I scanned the room, I saw Yeboah's mother lying in a heap at the altar and shaking as if she were having convulsions. I made my way to her where others were already in deep intercession for her, and I watched and prayed as what seemed like dark spirits came out of her.

As each one would come out, she would seem to rest for a few moments, then another would start, and eventually it looked like a light came on inside of her! She lit up and began to cry out "Jesus!" over and over! People were running and shouting as word spread that she had been delivered and was now worshipping Jesus.

Yeboah's eyes had been watching across the floor, underneath the feet of the worshippers, catching glimpses of her mother receiving her own miracle from God.

That mother's little girl was listening and watching as momma got free. When momma got free, baby got free!

The next morning we had gathered at the Prayer Center for our final morning session. This was when we would award the certificates of attendance and license nearly 100 workers to carry the Gospel into four countries! We were lounging in the church office while waiting to start when a very excited young man came rushing in shouting, "Pastor Stephen, you must come now!"

We jumped up and ran, following him into the sanctuary where I came to a sudden stop. I couldn't believe what I was seeing!

Yeboah was sitting up in a plastic chair and supporting her own weight! I was completely stunned as I came up beside the chair and looked over at her mother who was beaming with joy and smiling from ear to ear. She just kept saying what amounted to, "See what Jesus has done!"

People began to snap pictures as I knelt and spoke with them. I leaned over and gave Yeboah a kiss on the cheek as tears streamed down my face. She turned her face toward me and tried to smile! I said, "I love you!" Then she spoke for the first time in many weeks, "I love you, too!"

I cherish the pictures of those moments because, you see, I, too, have been a prisoner: to shame from more failures than I could count, to a reputation that folks around me just couldn't let me outlive, to character flaws that made me useless and unwanted by church leaders. My wife lived under my self imposed sentence of guilt and shame, as did my kids.

That morning, I was freed from a life of those imprisonments and self imposed punishments.

Where Did You Go, Gehazi?

Two years later, I would again be summoned from that same pastor's office.

We had returned for another leadership conference and nightly crusade meetings. This time, the crowds had grown tremendously! That little prayer center of 400 was now 2000! The nightly meetings saw people crowding into the building and spilling into the streets and woods all around the center. They had come for the same reason King Akumfi had wanted to see us; they wanted to see those who had been involved in the miracle two years before.

As I followed a young man to the sanctuary I knew I was in for something special. I rounded the corner and saw a beautiful twelve year-old girl standing in front of the platform. She was wearing a blue school uniform, and her hair was put up pretty. She was tall for her age and stood gracefully until she saw me. She came running toward me and jumped into my arms. I began to sob as Yeboah hugged me tight.

Her miracle had continued after we left. I had kept up with her through phone conversations with Bishop Thomas so I knew she was doing well, but nothing could have prepared me for the absolute joy of that moment. Her testimony had become so widespread that the family had allowed her to move in with the Bishop's family to attend school and to tell her story whenever possible.

Steve Price

Later that week, I was given the opportunity to baptize Yeboah and about a dozen of her friends in a muddy river in Ghana, Africa!

Where did you go, Steve? I went to grace!

Where Did You Go, Gehazi?

REMISSION

As Gehazi stood next to the King of Samaria, he might have been thinking, "How did I get here? Just awhile back I was a banished leper with a future destined for pain and loneliness, and now I'm testifying to the King about the works of Elisha and getting to help people that I couldn't help before."

How indeed? Just because you may have been one of the lepers that brought deliverance to Samaria doesn't excuse the fact that you're a leper and leprosy is contagious. You just don't get near anybody, especially the King, when you've got leprosy.

What could have happened to Gehazi that made this possible? Leviticus, chapter 13, that's what happened.

The rules said that when it appears a person has leprosy, they have to be examined by a priest. The priest would look at the stage your leprosy was in and declare your fate.

In most cases, leprosy begins with sores that spread and deepen, eventually becoming bloody and oozing. In this state, the leper is highly contagious and in those days, untreatable.

This may have been the condition of Gehazi's friends in the leper camp and it may have been the way he saw himself, but it's not what the Word says came upon him.

Leviticus 13 also gives instructions for leprosy that has gone into remission and a remedy for being returned to one's life.

"Or if the raw flesh turn again, and be changed unto white, he shall come unto the priest; And the priest shall see him: and, behold, if the plague be turned into white; then the priest shall pronounce him clean that hath the plague: he is clean."

So that's all Gehazi had to do from the time he had been found in his lie to Elisha. Go show yourself to the priest. If he hadn't condemned himself, he would have found the answer from the priest was that he was clean. Elisha had spoken a word over Gehazi that brought a condition to remind him of his wrong, but it would have also reminded him of something far greater and infinitely more powerful. Grace.

His leprosy came upon him and was immediately "white as snow" which would have been seen by the priest. And the remission of his condition would have given him life.

John the Baptist had preached a doctrine of

Where Did You Go, Gehazi?

repentance for the remission of sin. Jesus taught the disciples, before He ascended, that "repentance and remission of sins should be preached to all nations." The apostles taught the same doctrine that whoever believes in the name of Jesus would receive remission of sins.

It's that remission part that helps me see what the Lord has done for us.

I look at my life, and I see the ugly evidence of a life of sin and scars that will be there as long as I live, memories that rear their heads and an enemy that loves to remind me of what I used to be.

From the moment the Lord revealed to me that I had sinned against Him and asked me, as Elisha did Gehazi, "Where did you go, Gehazi," He had already provided a remedy, the remission of sin through the examination and pronouncement of the High Priest of our souls, Jesus.

Go, show yourself to the Priest today! You'll find the Word that revealed your sinful condition was already prepared to offer the remedy for that condition as well. Grace is more than able to restore to you the life that sin, guilt and shame have stolen from you.

"Seeing then that we have a great high priest, that is passed into the heavens, Jesus the Son of God, let us hold fast our profession. For we have not an high priest which cannot be touched with the feeling of our infirmities; but was in all points tempted like as we are, yet without sin. Let us therefore come boldly unto the throne of grace, that we may obtain mercy, and find grace to help in time of need" Hebrews 4:14 - 16 (KJV).

VICTORY IN JESUS

Isaiah 1:18

Come now, and let us reason together, saith the LORD: though your sins be as scarlet, they shall be as white as snow; though they be red like crimson, they shall be as wool (KJV).

One day those who have accepted what Jesus died to give will be allowed to stand in the presence of the King. What will give us that access? What will He see when He looks at us? If we have been covered by His sacrifice He will see a soul made white by the blood of the Lamb. Our conversation with God won't be about our works or how great we are, we will delight ourselves in declaring the words of that great hymn, Victory In Jesus!

Steve Price

Victory in Jesus.

I heard an old, old story
How a Savior came from glory
How He gave His life on Calvary
To save a wretch like me
I heard about His groaning
Of His precious blood's atoning
Then I repented of my sins
And won the victory

O victory in Jesus
My Savior, forever
He sought me and bought me
With His redeeming blood
He loved me ere I knew Him
And all my love is due Him
He plunged me to victory
Beneath the cleansing flood

ABOUT THE AUTHOR

Steve Price, is the campus pastor at War Hill South, a satellite fellowship of War Hill Christian Fellowship. He is an ordained minister with Christian Fellowship Ministerial Association, International, and has served as pastor of 2 other churches over the last 15 years. He has traveled throughout the United States, Ghana, Africa and Haiti preaching. He is an accomplished musician and songwriter, and is a published computer software developer. He lives in Winder, Georgia, with his wife Robin. Steve and Robin have two beautiful daughters, Heather and Courtney, a son-in-law, Jim, a grandson, Levi, and a dog and cat. This is his first book.

Contact information:WarHillSouth@gmail.com

https://www.facebook.com/graceforgehazi

Made in the USA
Lexington, KY
16 September 2018